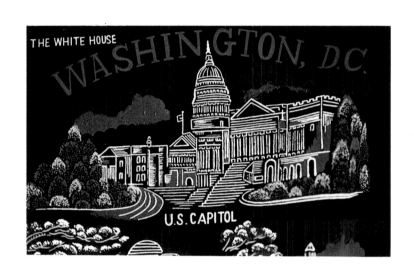

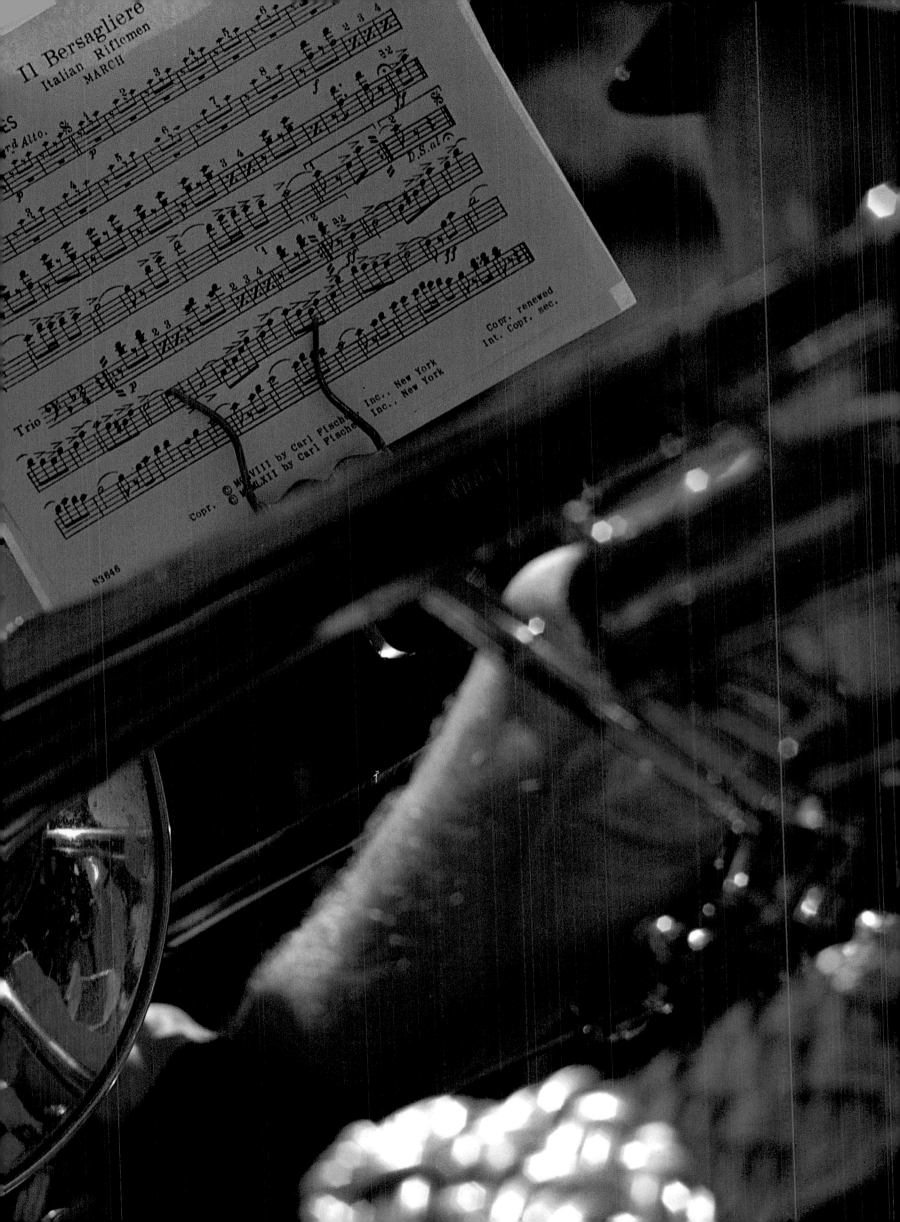

WASHING

TON, D.C.

Edited and Designed by JEAN-CLAUDE SUARÈS

Text by BILL HARRIS

Photo Editor and Coordinator: Deborah Augenblick

Photographs by

JOHN AIKENS ✦ MARIANNE BERNSTEIN ✦ MARIE L. BRIMBERG ✦ STEPHEN BROWN ✦ SONJA BULLATY ✦ KAY CHERNUSH

RON COLBROTH ✦ PAUL CONKLIN ✦ HENRI DAUMAN ✦ SALLY DIMARTINI ✦ GREGORY EDWARDS ✦ MICHAEL EVANS

ENRICO FERORELLI ✦ CHUCK FISHMAN ✦ ROGER FOLEY ✦ NICHOLAS FOSTER ✦ KENNETH GARRETT ✦ BURT GLINN

STEVEN GOTTLIEB ✦ DUDLEY GRAY ✦ DON HAMERMAN ✦ MAX HIRSHFELD ✦ MICHAEL HOYT ✦ LESLIE JEAN-BART

CYNTHIA JOHNSON ✦ EVERETT C. JOHNSON ✦ JAMES H. KARALES ✦ KELLY/MOONEY ✦ RICHARD LIPPMAN

FRED J. MAROON ✦ JOHN MCGRAIL ✦ HOWARD MILLARD ✦ MIKE MITCHELL ✦ JOHN NEUBAUER ✦ MARVIN E. NEWMAN

JEFF PERKELL ✦ DAVID ROBINSON ✦ SHEPARD SHERBELL ✦ NEAL SLAVIN ✦ JAMES A. SUGAR ✦ MICHAEL D. SULLIVAN

SIDNEY A. TABAK ✦ JONATHAN WALLEN ✦ FRED WARD ✦ ALEX WEBB ✦ WILLIAM S. WEEMS ✦ JEFF WILKES

HARRY N. ABRAMS, INC. ✦ PUBLISHERS ✦ NEW YORK

1 ✦ The five hundred thousand annual visitors to the Bureau of Engraving and Printing, the biggest moneymaking plant on earth, inevitably ask if they can take home souvenirs. The answer, just as inevitably, is "No!" But the thirty million visitors to Washington each year have plenty of other choices, including this pillow, symbolic, no doubt, of the soft life they're convinced their representatives lead. (Jonathan Wallen)

2–3 ✦ The Washington Monument doesn't open until eight on summer mornings, but if you could get to the top of this highest masonry structure in the world before the sun burns away the mist on the Mall, you'd find this view of the National Museum of American History, the National Museum of Natural History, and the National Gallery of Art along Madison Drive on the left, and the Department of Agriculture, followed by the buildings of the Smithsonian Institution, including the Hirshhorn Museum and the National Air and Space Museum, along Jefferson Drive on the right. The view is completed by the Capitol in the distance. (Fred J. Maroon)

8–9 ✦ The Capitol, the Washington Monument, and the Lincoln Memorial are all more than just landmarks on the horizon to Americans who come to Washington for the first time. They are a stirring experience difficult to forget, and the symbolism extends beyond first impressions for most. (Gregory Edwards)

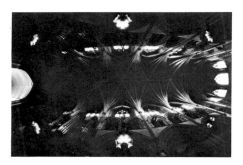

4–5 ✦ Since the day in 1907 when President Theodore Roosevelt laid its cornerstone, construction has never stopped on the Episcopalian Cathedral Church of St. Peter and St. Paul, also known as the Washington Cathedral or the National Cathedral. Except for the Cathedral of St. John the Divine in New York City, also unfinished, it is the largest cathedral in the United States. The arched Gothic ribs in the ceiling and most of the building's sculpture were carved on the site of Indiana limestone, the same material used in the structure itself. (Marie L. Brimberg)

10–11 ✦ A legend every schoolboy knows is the one about George Washington skimming a silver dollar across the Potomac River. This paper version of "One Silver Dollar" crossed the Atlantic Ocean in the pocket of Charles A. Lindbergh on his 1927 solo flight to Paris. It is part of the collection of the Library of Congress, which also contains a 1903 photograph taken by the Wright Brothers of the first flight. The Library's collection contained 76,945,360 items at the end of 1980; only 19,155,165 of those were books and pamphlets. (Jonathan Wallen)

6–7 ✦ Henry Bacon's design for the Lincoln Memorial is a happy combination of both Greek and Roman styles with a peristyle porch of Doric columns supporting an attic that would have been the pride of ancient Rome. Bacon used a bit of Greek trickery to fool your eye. The columns are tilted inward and they have a slight bulge to make them appear straight. (Don Hamerman)

12–13 ✦ If those gentlemen in the painting look surprised, it's not because they didn't expect to see the sculpture of Ulysses S. Grant by Franklin Simmons standing in the Capitol Rotunda. They're part of Colonel John Trumbull's painting of the day that General John Burgoyne surrendered 8,000 British troops at Saratoga, New York, in 1777. The painting is one of four in the Rotunda by Trumbull, who had served in the Revolutionary War and used many of its participants as his models. (Jonathan Wallen)

14–15 ◆ More than forty years before the Federal District became officially "the City of Washington" in 1791, a little town called Georgetown was a thriving place. In 1871, an act of Congress wiped out its independent government and made it a suburb within the city. Fifty years ago it was down-at-the-heels and ready for the wrecker's ball. Then Eleanor Roosevelt encouraged recycling the place, and the character of buildings like these along Wisconsin Avenue was saved to become part of the charm in one of the city's most fashionable, and expensive, neighborhoods.
(Kay Chernush)

16–17 ◆ Nearly everybody in Washington comes from some other place, and a great majority of them don't shake their roots. Ask them where they're from and they're more likely to say San Francisco, or Dallas, or any place else but Washington, even though this is their home. Increasingly, the answer is The People's Republic of China and, fortunately, some of the new arrivals have brought their talent for cooking with them. And with that, other Washingtonians are discovering at places such as the *House of Hunam* that there is more to Chinese food than chow mein and fried rice. (Jonathan Wallen)

18–19 ◆ Police protection is never far away in Washington. The combined numbers of the Capitol Police, the Washington Metropolitan Police, and the blue-helmeted Parks Police, along with the uniformed security forces of the various Federal departments, give the District one of the biggest per-capita police forces in the country. But until August 6, 1861, when Congress created the Metropolitan Police, law and order was in the hands of a few Federal marshalls and an auxiliary guard that worked only in the evenings to protect public buildings but not the public itself.
(Leslie Jean-Bart)

20–21 ◆ When work began on the Chesapeake and Ohio Canal in 1828, its promoters predicted it would make Washington one of the great industrial centers of the East. It didn't work out that way. The Baltimore and Ohio Railroad, begun the same year, took most of its business away. After the last boatload of coal was towed through it in 1924, the canal's owners began selling water to Georgetown factories. Fortunately, they didn't sell all of it, and its restored 184 miles of waterway allow nostalgic boat rides for tourists and a peaceful oasis for Washingtonians.
(John Neubauer)

22–23 ◆ Of all the things the government has given us, music is the one everyone agrees is a blessing. It was bestowed on the capital in 1801 with the creation of the U.S. Marine Corps Band, of which this red-jacketed trombone player is a member. In 1880, a native Washingtonian, John Philip Sousa, became its leader. The unit is the oldest military band in America and is always on hand for important Washington events. (Fred J. Maroon)

24–25 ◆ A local treasure that tourists and even some natives often miss is the Fountain of the Court of Neptune, set in a fifty-foot pool between the two sets of stairs leading to the main entrance of the Library of Congress. A bronze figure of Neptune dominates the group. On either side, a pair of Nereids ride prancing sea horses; Tritons blow jets of water from conch shells, forming crisscross patterns with jets of water sent out by frogs, turtles, and even a wriggling sea serpent. Blame it all on youthful exuberance. The heroic group was done by Roland Hinton Perry when he was twenty-seven years old. (Fred J. Maroon)

26–27 ◆ "Excuse me, can you tell me the way to the White House?" In spite of the fact that Washington was planned on a pattern that makes finding your way as simple as knowing that north-south streets are numbered, that east-west streets are lettered, and that avenues are generally named for states, there are enough variations to the rules to make a map indispensable to anyone who wants to be sure of not missing anything. (Chuck Fishman)

30–31 ◆ Its promoters call it "the Great American Flag" and claim it is the biggest flag in the world. Who can deny it? It measures 411 by 211 feet, about 2½ acres, and weighs 7 tons. It was first unfurled on the Mall by a small army of volunteers on Flag Day, June 14, 1980. The stars on the nylon taffeta banner, made in Evansville, Indiana, are 13 feet wide; the stripes are 16 feet tall. What price Old Glory? About $850,000. (John McGrail)

28–29 ◆ An aluminum mobile by Alexander Calder hangs from the huge skylight in the inner courtyard of I. M. Pei's 1978 East Building of the National Gallery of Art. When the National Gallery first opened, in 1941, it had an iron rule that it would never acquire art produced by a living artist. Fortunately, the policy died quickly and this building became inevitable. (Kenneth Garrett)

32–33 ◆ The Pope arrived on the Mall in one of the Sikorsky S-61 helicopters assigned to Presidential duty. The 16-person helicopter is the third in a series that has served the President since the Eisenhower administration. The White House staff refers to them as "White Tops" because of their paint job, which matches the Presidential jet, Air Force One. Based at the Marine facility at Quantico, Virginia, the helicopters have a range of 518 miles at a speed of 115 miles per hour. (Fred Ward/Black Star)

35–38 ◆ Imposing yet serene, the setting for the Capitol was meant to be an inspiration. And it doesn't fail. (Howard Millard)

CONTENTS

INTRODUCTION

Washington, D.C., is always compared to Paris, but it is more like Jerusalem, a mystical meeting place of the earthly and the divine. True, it was designed by a Frenchman, Pierre Charles L'Enfant, to look like Paris, with its own Champs Elysées and other wide tree-lined avenues emanating from a central point. True, it boasts a river like the Seine, with statues of muscular horsemen showing the way across stone bridges. But looks are only part of a city's description.

To Americans, a visit to Washington for the first time is a pilgrimage. A holy trek to the seat of government. An homage to the great men and women who shaped our past two hundred years. The White House and the Jefferson Memorial, for example, are revered with a silent awe only accorded to the Wailing Wall and the Dome of the Rock. The Arch of Triumph and the Eiffel Tower, Paris' best-known and most visited landmarks, celebrate, respectively, a series of military victories and a long forgotten World's Fair. But Washington's monuments celebrate great men such as Washington, Jefferson, and Lincoln, who sacrificed themselves to see a dream come true just like Herod, who rebuilt the Temple two thousand years ago in the hope of seeing his people united.

Washington is considered the custodian of our national shrines, but then, like Jerusalem, it is also the city of tragic divisions—in reality two cities. On one hand, it is the city of light-skinned rulers who make rules and send soldiers to fight in other countries; on the other hand, the city of darker-skinned people, including Moslems, who find themselves trapped in an urban maze where progress is slow to come and desperation slow to disappear. This book is about a discovery: the third Washington—the Washington of the camera which knows no prejudice and never passes judgment, linking past and present, summer and winter, day and night, and even Black and White. In fact, the camera has been eyeing Washington in much the same way since the 1840's. It is the theme of this book.

Stacks of firewood, a greenhouse, and backyard privies serve private homes along
F Street in this 1846 daguerrotype of the Patent Office.

Thousands of photographs in the Library of Congress document every aspect of Washington's official and everyday life for nearly 140 years. There are photographs of every important event that has ever taken place there. You may find, for example, photographs of every inauguration since James K. Polk's in 1845 (only five years after the birth of photography). And you may see photographs that describe in minute detail the metamorphosis of such buildings as the White House and the Capitol—their construction, reconstruction, repair, and two centuries worth of tenants.

If you put yourself in the shoes of photographers, however, you will discover a strange phenomenon: it seems that they've not only photographed the same events and buildings every day of the year, but they've always chosen to see the city from the same time-tested spots. The most common expression of Washington is the view of the Capitol from afar. Since it appears from every vantage point, be it Arlington or Georgetown, its entire circumference has been carefully recorded. Over the decades marshes and swamps have been replaced by asphalt, but the sight is still reassuring: through world wars, economic crises, and even Watergates, the dome rises solidly in the center.

Washington knows more celebrations than any other city. Not just local celebrations, but the national ones, and most important the one that happens every four years, the inauguration of the President. There are parades and inaugural balls and fireworks fill the sky above the Capitol as they did one hundred years ago. It is also the city of speeches, press conferences, and filibusters, when a single individual is allowed to hold a large group of people captive as he repeats the campaign promises that got him to Washington. It seems as if every day in Washington someone is doing just that—holding an audience captive solely with hot air as bait.

Above: Construction on the Capitol dome in the early 1860's as it looked during Abraham Lincoln's first term.

The earliest known photo of the Capitol was made in about 1846 showing the wooden dome designed by Charles Bulfinch.

An 1846 daguerrotype of the White House as it looked when
James K. Polk lived there.

WASHINGTON MOTORCYCLE CLUB, SOCIABILITY

Back in 1919, before the days of power lawnmowers, a herd of
sheep kept the White House lawn manicured.

Thirty-five members of the Washington Motorcycle Club, eight passengers, and six bystanders pose in front of the White House for a group
portrait on October 31, 1915. The occasion is the Club's annual Sociability Run to Baltimore, Maryland. The photographer, S. Schutz, specialized in
wide-frame group portraits typical of the period (Courtesy Mark Segal)

BALTIMORE MD. OCTOBER. 31, 1915.

There are no more Potomac longboats, the two-masted barges used to carry cordwood from Maryland and Virginia to the Chesapeake Bay, but the Potomac River will always be the center of summer activities. It now boasts thousands of pleasure boats of every kind. Here self-consciousness about ostentatious vehicles doesn't exist, though wealth is still being flaunted with cabin cruisers much larger than they need to be. Only the magnificent *Sequoia*, the Presidential yacht, has been sold to the highest bidder by President Jimmy Carter, presumably as a measure of austerity but more likely because of his legendary seasickness.

Unlike other places where buildings are torn down to make room for new ones, buildings here are renovated on the outside and redecorated on the inside. Every single style of urban architecture that's ever been used in America is represented: Colonial, Georgian, Romanesque-Revival, Victorian, Neoclassical, Gothic-Revival, Modern. All are lived in. Even the tiny brick houses that were built two hundred years ago for slaves have been preserved.

The buildings, the river, the Capitol, the other landmarks, and all the important events taking place here are continuously recorded by those who make a living doing so. Many belong to the White House Press Photographers Association, others work for the *Washington Post* or *National Geographic* magazine. But the professionals are a minority because thousands of tourists every day aim their cameras at a friend or member of their family standing on the steps of the Capitol or by the White House fence. They want a memento just as their fathers and grandfathers had in a family album of long ago. Photos of sacred places, the Wailing Wall, John F. Kennedy's tomb, the Vatican, are serious pictures for which you stand erect. You can look at the camera and smile, but no horseplay is allowed, as in Paris.

Turn the pages here and watch Washington refuse to change. The sun rises again and again over the monuments; crowds gather to hear a lone speaker or a man conducting an orchestra; and the city celebrates its new leader every four years without fail. Winter will come again and again to remind you that Washington is near Yankee territory, and summer will find its children diving in the river as they do in the South.

Thank the camera for making it all possible. Large box cameras that were carried by men in tall, black silk hats and tails, and small cameras held up by men in checkered jackets and a reassuring feeling in their hearts. J.C. SUARÈS

Above: When this capstone was removed from the construction
shed and hoisted 555 feet and 5⅛ inches to the top of the Washington
Monument in 1884, it became the world's tallest masonry structure.

Mark Twain said it looked like "a factory chimney with the top
broken off." Construction had stopped on the Washington Monument
for twenty-two years, but started again in time for the Brady Studio to
take this picture in 1880.

WASHINGTON MONUMENT, FROM THE POTOMAC, WASHINGTON, D.C.

In memory of my trip

K. Biltz

THE WASHINGTON MONUMENT, WASHINGTON, D.C.

Though am not in Washington will send you one of its pictures — I find that Horace H. is in Washington you remember I told you thought he was in Conn. He didn't stay there long I guess — lovingly Constance

W-6. ILLUST. POST CARD CO., N.Y.

4/12/05

PHOTO-ELECTROTYPE ENG. CO., N.Y.   PUB. BY MRS. HOWARD GREY DOUGLAS, WASHINGTON, D.C.

WASHINGTON MONUMENT

March 5, '05.

Top left: Postcards of the Washington Monument outsell all others. They were manufactured even before the monument was completed. The postmark on the back of this card is from May 9, 1907, when it cost one penny to mail it. The inscription on the front reads: "In memory of my trip . . . K. Biltz." Top right: A card of the Washington Monument of 1905, published by one Mrs. Howard Grey Douglas. Bottom left: This card, manufactured by the Illustrated Post Card Co., New York, was addressed to Miss Hannie Haud of Bridgehampton, New York, on November 12, 1905. Originally, it was handtinted, a common technique before the advent of color offset printing. Bottom right: "The Washington Monument by Night," a postcard made for nearly thirty years by the B. S. Reynolds Co. The pool and the reflection of the monument have disappeared to make way for a cement road.

DAWN

When the sun rises along the East Coast, people in Boston and New York turn over to grab another forty winks. Their day doesn't begin until nine. In Chicago, Houston, and Los Angeles it is still night. But the people who represent the Americans in those cities in Washington are usually well on their way before the sun breaks over the horizon. Many begin their workday at seven; others precede their workday in breakfast conferences or in traffic jams. Even people who aren't morning persons by nature get the spirit. And why not? It's a beautiful time of day here.

50 ◆ The first Washington organization to shed light on America's past was the Smithsonian Institution, established by Congress in 1846 with money willed by James Smithson, an Englishman who never saw the United States but whose tomb is in this building known as "The Castle." It was designed by James Renwick and built in 1855. (William S. Weems)

51 ◆ Sleeping under bridges is frowned upon in the District of Columbia, but anyone who sees a sunrise from under the Theodore Roosevelt Bridge may have the added pleasure of being on the 88-acre Theodore Roosevelt Island, a nature preserve with three-and-a-half miles of trails through forest, swamp, and marsh. In the late eighteenth century, the island was the summer estate of General John Mason, son of George Mason, the great Virginia patriot. (Ron Colbroth)

52–53 ◆ Long before the rising sun adds touches of gold to the White House facade, an impressive percentage of the more than three hundred people who work there are already on the job. The uniformed guard is part of a visible unit of the Secret Service, a force created by the Treasury Department to stem the tide of counterfeiting during the Civil War. The Secret Service was assigned to protect the President in 1901, after the assassination of President William McKinley. Before then, the President was officially unprotected in spite of the fact that Presidents Garfield and Lincoln had been shot to death while in office. (William S. Weems)

54–55 ◆ The seventeenth-century immigrants who laid out new towns in New England established a tradition of lining their streets with trees. The idea was carried south and west as the country grew. But no American city is as admired for its shade trees as Washington. More than seventy thousand that line streets like this one on Capitol Hill were planted during the Grant administration in the 1870's, when the District of Columbia was temporarily made a territory administered by a governor, "Boss" Alexander Shepherd; he also gave the city many of its paved streets and most of its sanitation system. (Mike Mitchell)

56 ◆ The Capitol Rotunda, 180 feet from floor to canopy and 96 feet across at the base, is embellished with a fresco by an Italian refugee, Constantino Brumundi. The cast-iron dome that encloses it was designed by Thomas U. Walter, a Philadelphia architect. It replaced Charles Bulfinch's copper-sheathed wooden dome, which was removed in 1855. The area under the old dome was the setting for exhibitions that had all the trappings of a flea market where entrepreneurs sold their exhibits, which ranged from kitchen gadgets to hair ribbons to furniture. (Stephen Brown)

57 ✦ The Hirshhorn Museum's Sculpture Garden provides a frame for the National Air and Space Museum in the form of a sculpture by Alexander Calder. The institutions are strange next door neighbors—the Air and Space Museum seems to be made entirely of windows, but the Hirshhorn is all walls; the only window in the building is on the third floor. (Steven Gottlieb)

58 ✦ The sign says this is Sholl's *New* Cafeteria, and the location (at 1900 K St. NW) is new. But there has been a Sholl's in Washington for more than fifty years. Ask owner Evan Sholl why he's been so successful and he'll tell you about hard work (thirteen hours a day from 7:00 A.M every day but Sunday), steady, loyal customers (about a million a year), low prices (try spending more than $3 for a meal), and old-time religion (served up in the form of mottoes on little signs all over the place). (Sally DiMartini)

59 ✦ Thomas Jefferson was one of the first in America to speak out against slavery and a quotation from his 1774 *Summary View of the Rights of British America* is inscribed on one of the walls of his Memorial: "God who gave us life gave us liberty at the same time. Indeed I tremble for my country when I reflect that God is just, that His justice cannot sleep forever. Commerce between master and slave is despotism. Nothing is more certainly written in the book of fate than that these people are to be free. . . ." (Kay Chernush)

60–61 ✦ From the turn of the century through the 1949 inauguration of President Harry S. Truman, the B & O railroad yards outside Union Station were filled with sleeping cars during inaugurals to accommodate the overflow from the city's hotels. Most of the rail traffic today is by Amtrak coaches and Metroliners, which make the trip from New York in about three hours. Trains like the Night Owl from Boston, arriving at eight in the morning, still provide sleeping accommodations, but nobody pays for the privilege of sleeping in the railroad yards anymore. (Max Hirshfeld)

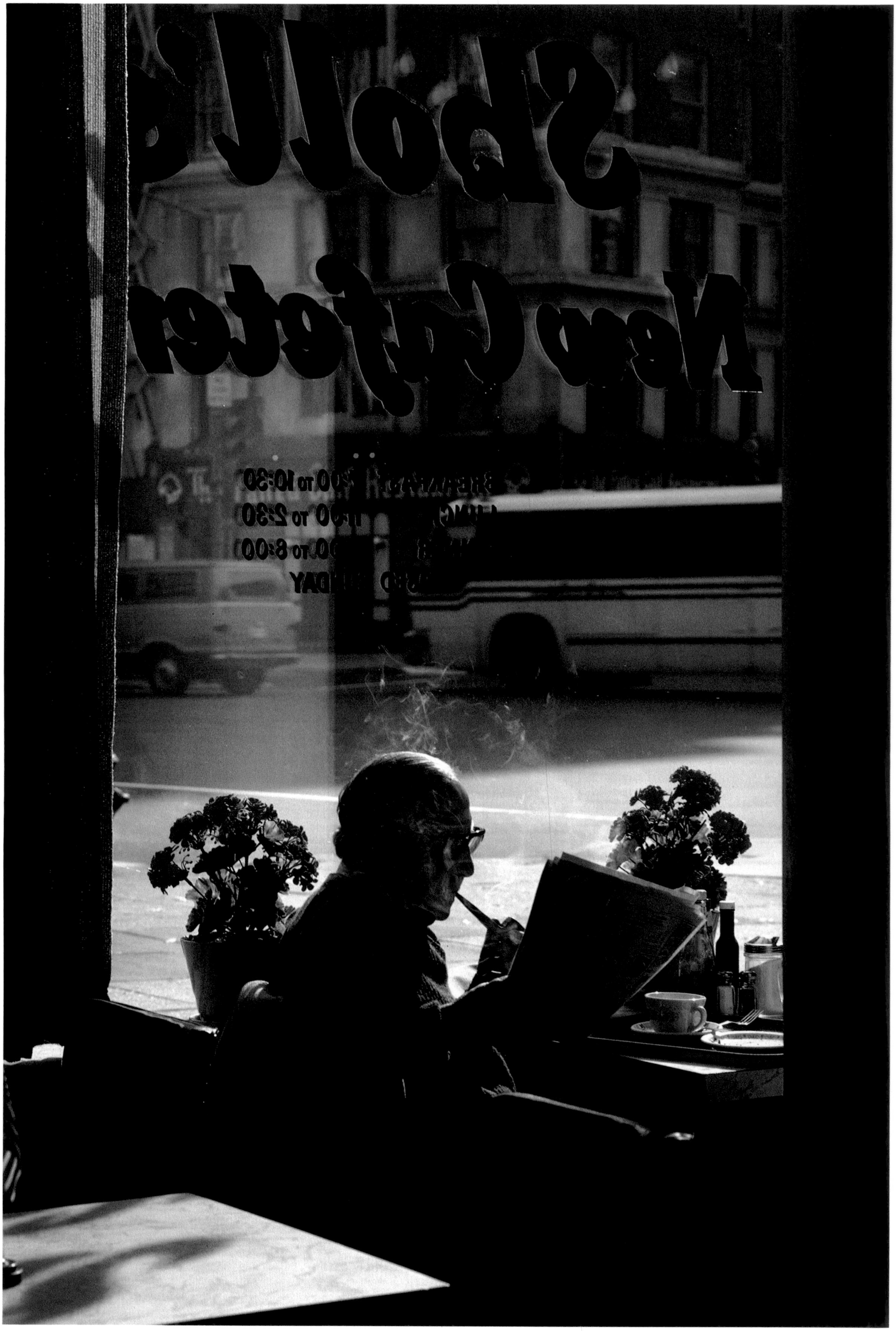

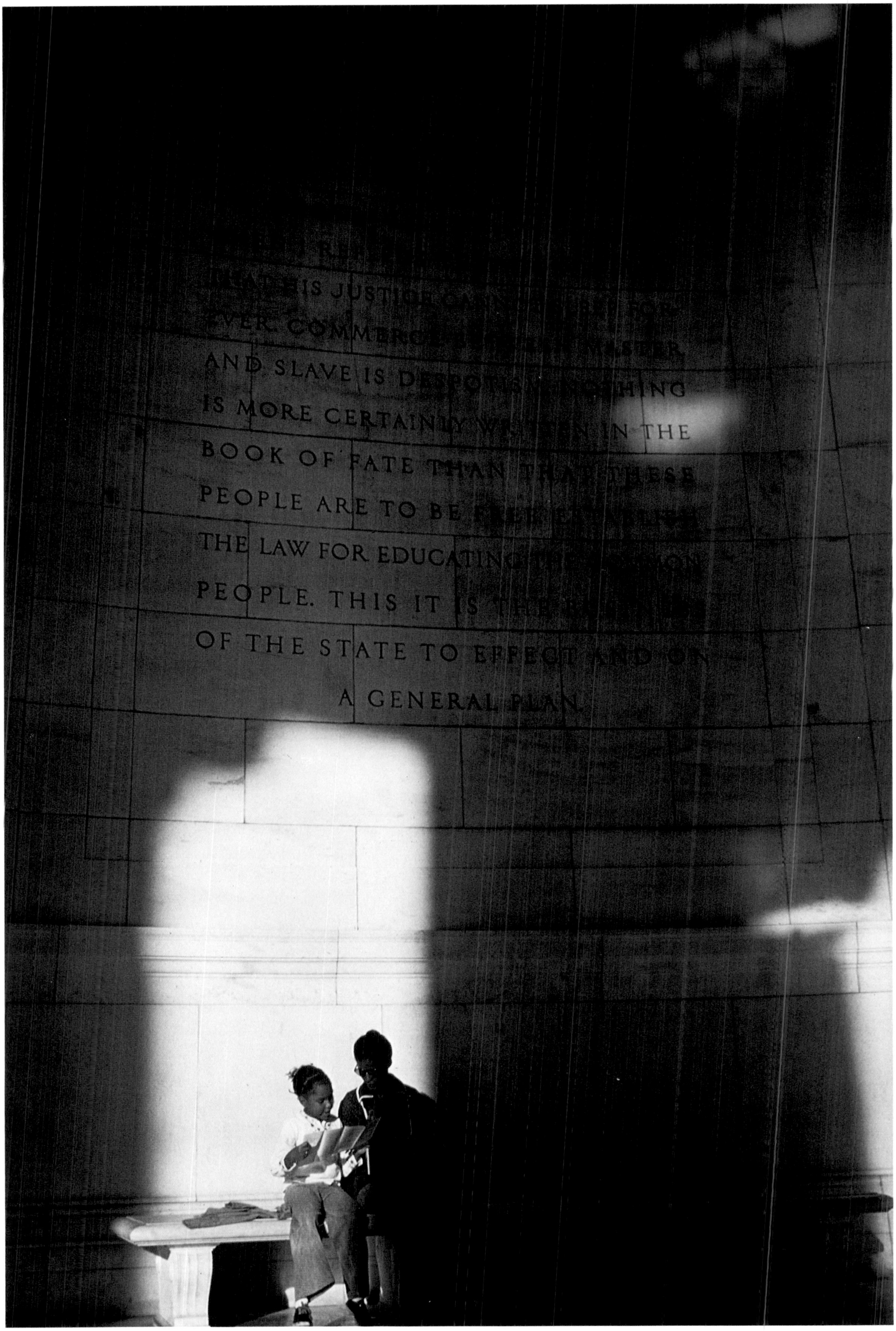

© KAY CHERNUSH

CULTURE

Among the myths about Washington, the most prevalent one for generations was that it is a cultural wasteland. The only theater outsiders knew about was Ford's Theater where Lincoln was shot; the only music, they thought, was provided by the Marine Band. But, fortunately for Washingtonians, the myth is much less persistent now that Washington's cultural institutions have heaped fame on themselves as well as their city; people are beginning to visit here just to share them.

62 ✦ In 1897, the Library of Congress moved from this room in the center of the Capitol's West Front to its new building across the street.

63 ✦ Alexander Calder, who made this stabile on display in the National Gallery's East Building, called the work *Obus*. Though the operating expenses of the National Gallery are provided by Congress, the $95-million building and the collection inside didn't cost the taxpayers a dime. The East Building was a gift of the Mellon Family Foundation, following the tradition of Andrew Mellon, who made a gift of his art collection and the West Building to the American people in 1937. (John McGrail)

64–65 ✦ In 1981, 1,497,698 people took the free guided tour of the Capitol. The American citizens among them own the place and the Capitol Guide Force reports most of them take more than a casual interest in its upkeep. Making sure they have nothing to complain about is the job of the 180-person maintenance staff that includes painters and plumbers, carpenters and electricians. The job of cleaning and restoring the priceless works of art in the building is handled by professional conservators brought in periodically. (Jonathan Wallen)

66–67 ✦ The mural painter John de Rosen specializes in ecclesiastical art. He painted the murals for Pope Pius XI's private chapel at his villa in Castel Gandolfo in the 1930's and later did a 72-by-35-foot mosaic, *Christ in Majesty*, for Washington's National Shrine of the Immaculate Conception. The painting of him at work on a panel that was given to Pope John Paul II is by Washington artist Frank Wright, a neighbor of de Rosen's in a studio building across from the National Portrait Gallery. (Sidney A. Tabak)

62

68 ◆ Andrew Mellon's collection of 121 Old Masters became the National Gallery's permanent collection; this included twenty-one from the Hermitage in Leningrad that he had bought in 1931 from the Soviet government for seven million dollars, money they needed to finance a Five-Year Plan. Today, students can secure thirty-day permits to copy pictures in the West Building (copying is not permitted in the East Building) as a means of perfecting their own technique. Only ten copyists are allowed in the Gallery on a given day, and their copies must be at least two inches smaller or larger than the original. Here is Rembrandt's *The Mill* in two versions. (Don Hamerman)

69 ✦ If the face of Antor Fugger is familiar, you may have seen it in the Kress Collection at the National Gallery—as done by the sixteenth-century German painter Hans Maler. The person hiding behind it is a member of the Gallery staff assigned to aid a photographer in making a reproduction for publication. Books, prints, cards, and other items with quality reproductions of the Gallery's collections are offered for sale in the Gallery itself. (Sonja Bullaty)

70 ✦ National Cathedral is obviously the best setting in town for
medieval-style singers. It has also been the setting for modern dance,
opera, drama, even an oompah band. On one occasion, seven hundred
musicians gathered for an impressive performance of Mahler's Eighth
Symphony; on another, the U.S. Army Brass Ensemble filled the nave
with its special sound. Once a year, in the fall, the Annual Open House
features demonstrations of stone-cutting, stained-glass work, and
needlepoint and includes music, mimes, movies, and even a carrousel
outside. (William S. Weems)

71 ✦ The Music Division of the Library of Congress has more than 3.6
million music scores from the classics to recent rock and roll. The
collection also contains two violins, a viola, and a cello made by the
seventeenth-century Italian craftsman Antonio Stradivari. The instruments
are occasionally played by such groups as the Juilliard String Quartet,
who participate in a regular concert series begun in 1925 in the Library's
Elizabeth Sprague Coolidge Auditorium. (Jonathan Wallen)

72 ✦ Rock Creek Park, a nature preserve of 1,800 acres, has picnic groves and bridle paths, two golf courses, a planetarium, and a nature center. It has a log cabin, the only one in Washington, brought here from California, and a restored water mill that still grinds flour and corn meal. But for many, the Park is at its best on a cool summer evening when the New York City Ballet and others give performances at the Carter Barron Amphitheater. (Fred J. Maroon)

73 ✦ In the first ten years since the John F. Kennedy Center for the Performing Arts opened with the premiere performance of Leonard Bernstein's *Mass* on September 8, 1971, more than forty million people have visited the Center. More than a third of them were ticket holders for one of the more than ten thousand performances on one of the stages there. Though the average rate of ticket sales is about 80 percent of capacity, an impressive figure for any cultural enterprise, many performances are sold out well in advance, as was the case for this performance of Beethoven's *Fidelio* by the Vienna State Opera. (Enrico Ferorelli/Wheeler Pictures)

74–75 ✦ The 19,000-seat Capital Centre, thirty miles out of town in Landover, Maryland, is ordinarily where you go to watch the Washington Capitals play hockey or the Bullets play basketball, but on the night of January 19, 1981, it was the scene of a two-hour celebrity-studded gala celebrating the inauguration of Ronald Reagan as 40th President of the United States. The televised show featured such stars as Ben Vereen and a formally dressed audience who had paid $150 each to see it live. The following night the new President made the rounds of eight inaugural balls which were covered by forty TV cameras and a technical crew of 450. (Fred Ward)

INTERIORS

First impressions of Washington usually revolve around the vistas, the sculpture, the variety of architectural styles. But the lasting impressions are created by the city's interiors, ranging from lavish to simple, but always impressive. They were meant to be impressive, to let you know that this is an important place where important things are happening. Most of the best Washington interiors are easily accessible, to be enjoyed and admired by more than just the people who work there.

76 ✦ The Pension Building is decorated with red, white, and blue bunting for an inaugural ball, probably for Grover Cleveland in 1893.

77 ✦ First-time visitors to Georgetown Park, an enclosed shopping mall on M Street near the C&O Canal, usually ask what was there before the shops, boutiques, and a branch of Garfinckle's department store appeared. The answer is that the site was mostly open space. The fountain, the light fixtures, and other artifacts were created for the mall, which opened in September 1981. Each of its three levels exits to the street thanks to a trick of topography that puts one at the level of the Canal, the next higher on Wisconsin Avenue, and the top on M Street. There are three levels of parking below it and three more of condominium apartments being developed above it. (Jeff Perkell)

78 ✦ Just in time for America's Bicentennial celebration in 1976, the
District of Columbia unveiled the first leg of its Metrorail subway
system, and work on the five lines that will become the full system hasn't
stopped since. The projected cost is above eight billion, but Washington
people are well aware of the difference between estimates and final costs.
The growing system penetrates the Maryland and Virginia suburbs.
(Fred Ward/Black Star)

79 ✦ If you've seen the Pantheon in Rome, say the designers of Metrorail, you should recognize the ceilings in the stations. The coffered ceilings reflect light coming from below the floor where the arch vanishes under the platform. When Metrorail is completely built, there will be eighty-six underground stations, each with platforms six hundred feet long—the length of three blocks above ground. (Marvin E. Newman)

80 ✦ When Franklin D. Roosevelt arrived in Washington in 1933, he brought a lot of revolutionary ideas with him. One of them was to remove the dome from the Library of Congress. "It's out of tune," he said. Fortunately the idea fell on deaf ears and Edwin H. Blashfield's murals, *Human Understanding*, in the dome's lantern, and the 150-foot *Progress of Civilization*, which forms its collar, were rescued, as were the sixteen bronze statues on the gallery balustrade, including Paul Wayland Bartlett's *Michelangelo*. (Jonathan Wallen)

81 ✦ The sculpture of Lincoln in the Capitol Rotunda is by Vinnie Ream, the first woman to get a United States commission for a work of art. "She talked pretty girlish talk to those impotent iron-clad old politicians," said Mark Twain, "and they told her to go, take a room in the Capitol, build Mr. Lincoln and be happy." (Jonathan Wallen)

82 ✦ A rampaging Republican? You'd better hope not! This creature weighs twelve tons. It's the biggest African elephant ever shot, brought here from the wilds of Angola to the Rotunda of the National Museum of Natural History. The museum's collection in botany, anthropology, geology, and zoology includes more than 48,000,000 specimens. (Jonathan Wallen)

83 ✦ The mahogany reading desks that circle the central distributing desk in the Reading Room of the Library of Congress accommodate three hundred persons. The arches that support the 125-foot dome are held up by columns of red Numidian marble. The eight semicircular stained-glass windows above the sixteen portrait sculptures in the gallery contain seals of the contiguous forty-eight states. All eight have the Great Seal of the United States at the top. (Marvin E. Newman)

84–85 ✦ An average of ten million visitors a year make the Smithsonian's National Air and Space Museum the world's busiest. A Douglas DC-3, the workhorse of air travel before the days of big jets, is the biggest object in an exhibit that includes the Wright Brothers' first plane and the space capsule that took the Apollo II mission to the moon. The building also houses the Albert Einstein Spacearium, the most technically perfect planetarium ever built. It was a Bicentennial birthday present to the people of the United States from the people of the Federal Republic of Germany. (Alex Webb/Magnum)

86–87 ✦ Depending on the season and the size of the budget, the National Parks Service has a staff of about a hundred people assigned to the job of keeping the monuments along the Mall shipshape and Bristol fashion. Three of them work full time at the Jefferson Memorial, keeping the marble floors shiny and maintaining the wool carpeting in the area created for access by handicapped persons. (Jonathan Wallen)

88–89 ✦ The eighty-foot Corinthian columns in the Old Pension Building are the tallest of their kind ever built. Even the Romans weren't this ambitious. They frame Washington's biggest interior space, a 30,000 square-foot room eight Presidents have chosen for their inaugural balls. The Pension Bureau, now part of the Veterans Administration, was the building's first tenant in 1883. They reached upper floors by elevator, the first ever used in a major Washington building. (Michael D. Sullivan)

90 ✦ The original White House plan by James Hoban intended the Green Room to be used as a dining room. Today it serves as a parlor. Thomas Jefferson used it as a dining room and furnished it with a round table so there would be no questions about who should sit at the head. He also added a revolving door with shelves so that servants didn't have to leave the pantry to get such new delicacies as ice cream, waffles, and macaroni into the room . (Shepard Sherbell)

91 ✦ The Rembrandt Peale portrait of Thomas Jefferson (here hidden by the chandelier) hanging on the north wall of the oval Blue Room in the White House was the best-known likeness of the third president when he lived there. The furnishings were ordered from Paris by the fifth president, James Monroe. Among them, a pier table that features a mirror on the bottom so women could adjust their floor-length skirts was rescued from a storage room by Mrs. John F. Kennedy in 1962 when other furnishings were carefully reproduced to return the room to its nineteenth-century elegance. (Shepard Sherbell)

92–93 ✦ Back in the days when mules towed barges through the C&O Canal there was a building in Georgetown that was a combination veterinary hospital and foundry making the shoes mules wore. Today, that 1856 building has been converted into a restaurant, and a new collection of buildings, built in the mid-1970's, complements it as a small shopping complex called The Foundry. For all its nineteenth-century feeling, reflections in the shop windows create an abstraction very much of the twentieth. (Kay Chernush)

THE CAPITOL

In 1791, after he explored the spot called Jenkins Hill, Pierre Charles L'Enfant said it was "a pedestal waiting for a great monument." Congress agreed and offered a $500 prize for the best design for that monument, a new Capitol building. William Thornton, an amateur architect, won it, and construction began. He was replaced in 1802 by a professional, Benjamin Henry Latrobe, who expanded but didn't change the plan. Three years after the British burned the building in 1814, the great Boston architect, Charles Bulfinch, took over and thirty-nine years after Thornton spent his $500, the building, looking very much like his original idea, was open for the nation's business. It has been expanded and altered since. The present dome was added in the 1860's; the East Front extension was finished in time to usher in the 1960's.

94 ✦ Pennsylvania Avenue from Treasury Plaza in 1908, when automobiles began joining the streetcar and carriage traffic.

95 ✦ A sculpture by Alexander Liberman in the garden of the National Gallery's East Building accents the geometry of the structure itself and gives a futuristic touch to the classical lines of the Capitol dome. I. M. Pei's edifice seems at home on the Mall, even though it is surrounded by buildings inspired by ideas from another time, another place.
(Paul Conklin)

96–97 ✦ Those bronze Civil War cavalrymen by Henry Merwin Shrady have been leaping out of the shrubbery at the Mall's east end since 1916 when they joined an equally impressive artillery group placed about two hundred feet to the south four years earlier. Four years later the grouping was crowned with an equestrian statue of General Ulysses S. Grant. The memorial was officially dedicated on Grant's hundredth birthday, April 27, 1922, by Vice President Calvin Coolidge (President Harding was in Ohio dedicating Grant's birthplace), two weeks after the sculptor's death.
(Jonathan Wallen)

98 ✦ A 1910 Act of Congress, aimed at keeping Washington a city of
open vistas, prevents builders, with very few exceptions, from making
their buildings more than twenty feet higher than the width of the street.
The maximum height in most parts of the city is 130 feet. But there are
times, especially when the vista is from the shore of the Anacostia River,
when some people wish for a way to screen the view of the builders
themselves. (John Neubauer)

99 ✦ In 1791, when George Washington sent Pierre Charles L'Enfant's plan for the Federal City to Congress, he wrote: "The Grand Avenue connecting the President's Palace and the Federal House will be most magnificent & most convenient." When President Kennedy used it as the traditional route to the White House from his 1961 inauguration, he found Pennsylvania Avenue convenient but not all that magnificent. Because of his efforts to upgrade it, there was a serious plan to change its name to Kennedy Avenue after his assassination in 1963, a plan that was dropped in favor of making the Kennedy Center his only memorial in the capital. (John Aikens)

100 ✦ Back in the days before we all became jet-setters, such railroads as the Atlantic Coast Line, the Pennsylvania, the Seaboard Air Line, the Richmond, Fredericksburg and Potomac, the Chesapeake and Ohio, and the Baltimore and Ohio all came together at Washington's Union Station. Passengers who arrived aboard the more than two hundred trains a day were treated to this view of the Capitol as they stepped outside. Today, the number of trains has dwindled to about fifty a day, mostly under the Amtrak banner, but including three Conrail runs from Baltimore, and several B&O commuter trains from the Maryland suburbs. (Fred J. Maroon)

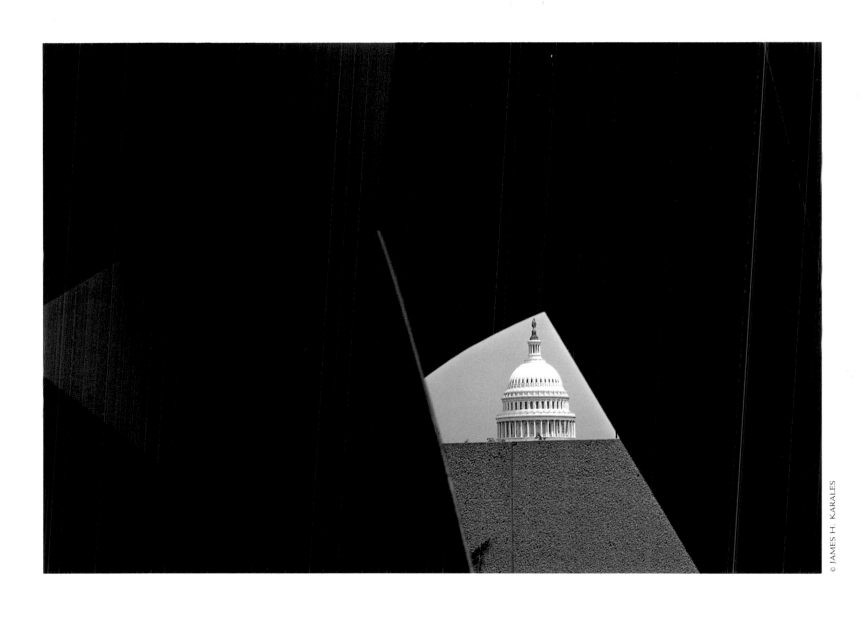

101 ✦ An Alexander Calder work in the Sculpture Garden of the Hirshhorn Museum is part of one of the largest collections of art ever assembled by a private individual. Joseph H. Hirshhorn gave his art, more than two thousand sculptures and four thousand paintings, to the government in 1966 because, as he put it, "I could not have done what I did in any other country." He made a fortune in the stock market before he was thirty, less than twenty years after arriving at Ellis Island as a Latvian immigrant. More came later when he gained control of a uranium conglomerate. (James H. Karales)

102 ✦ At various times as late as the 1880's, serious proposals were made
to move the seat of government away from Washington, and some
Midwestern cities like St. Louis spent small fortunes on big presentations
to promote their cause. On days like this one, after the blizzard of 1966,
a lot of people find themselves wishing a city in Florida or southern
California had put in a bid and won. (Fred J. Maroon)

103 ✦ In 1814 a British force attacked Washington and burned every
public building in town except the Post Office. It took more than five
years to rebuild the Capitol, during which time Congress met in a
temporary brick structure on part of the present site of the Supreme
Court Building. In 1817, James Monroe took his oath of office on the
steps of the temporary building. These days, most of the violence on
Capitol Hill is verbal, and exploding shells are reserved for celebrations
like this one on July 4, 1976. (Howard Millard)

104–105 ✦ As a city that is supposed to represent all of America, it is
only fitting that Washington has joined the national trend for physical
fitness. But runners and joggers in Washington have a big advantage over
their counterparts in other sections of the country: there are more good
places to run here. And when you consider that so many people had to
run so hard to get here in the first place, it's no wonder so many
Washingtonians are so addicted to it. (William S. Weems)

CAMERAS

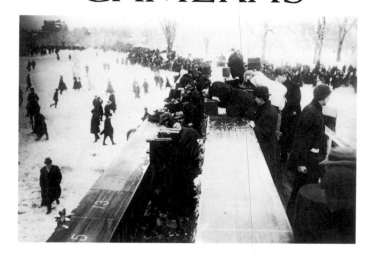

It may be the most photographed city in America. In addition to hundreds who make their living with cameras, recording the great and small moments of history that happen here every day, tourists visiting Washington take home part of the American Dream in the form of personal pictures. As anyone who has a camera knows, it's like a contagious disease. And Washingtonians are far from immune to it. Members of Congress, office clerks, and every type of civil servant have caught the bug.

106 ✦ On March 9, 1909, the day William Howard Taft was inaugurated, photographers had to clear snow away from the special platform they used to record the festivities.

107 ✦ Crime photographers? Probably not. There are picture opportunities in every direction in Washington and it would seem criminal not to take advantage of them. Now that good cameras are available in pocket size, it's possible to keep building your picture collection even when you're on the job. (Fred Ward/Black Star)

108–109 ✦ Watching people is one of Washington's great pleasures, and very often the people you're watching are there to entertain you. They play music, do magic tricks, dance, and juggle. And some of the street entertainers are very good mimes, like this one on the Capitol grounds who made it part of her act to ape the movements of photographers recording a rally of supporters of the Equal Rights Amendment. (Richard Lippman)

110 ✦ It's a good idea to keep smiling when you explore Washington. You never know when someone is snapping your picture. Don't worry about it, though. More than likely it's another explorer like yourself. And you *do* have an interesting face, after all. (Neal Slavin)

111 ✦ "I doubt if Barnum's circus has housed as many species as has been in our government," said the humorist Will Rogers. They got even by putting his statue in the Capitol. Every now and then strange things happen outside that make you wonder if he was really only fooling. (Nicholas Foster)

112–113 ✦ Except for George Washington, who was inaugurated as President in New York, the other five Presidents who preceded Andrew Jackson took their oaths of office in the Senate Chamber, probably before audiences smaller than this battery of photographers who went to a good deal of trouble to secure permits to record the Carter inaugural in 1977. The pageantry they photographed is a legacy of the Jackson idea that public ceremonies ought to be shared by as much of the public as possible. (Fred J. Maroon)

114 ✦ When Britain's Prince Charles was invited to the White House for
a private dinner in May 1981, pastry chef Roland Mesnier created this
dessert in the form of a crown made of ice cream with three feathers, part
of the Prince's coat of arms, inserted in the center. "Mrs. Reagan wanted
the feathers to be as fine as real feathers," he recalled. It took him five
attempts to create the illusion in blown sugar. So White House executive
chef Henry Haller, on the left, and Hans Raffert, behind the other
camera, wanted to capture it on film for you.
(Michael Evans/White House Photo)

115 ✦ Who's that coming down the street? It's none other than West
German Chancellor Helmut Schmidt. These people were giving
him a warm welcome and getting good pictures in return as he
arrived at the White House on a perfect day in May 1981.
(Cynthia Johnson/White House Photo)

THE POTOMAC

It begins in the Allegheny Mountains and wanders down past Washington to the Chesapeake Bay. Captain John Smith, of the Jamestown Colony, was the first to sail up the river as far as the present site of Washington, in 1608. Though he was enthusiastic in his report, nobody bothered to follow him until 1634, when the second Lord Baltimore arrived to explore his Maryland grant. He found the Indians hostile and placed his colony downriver, leaving the territory around Washington to be developed by aristocratic planters, mostly Virginians.

116 ✦ Anyone who falls into the Potomac today is required to get a tetanus shot. But back in 1923, special diving platforms encouraged people to leap into the clean, cool water.

117 ✦ The spires of Georgetown University, the Potomac Boat Club, and a boat powered by muscle conjure up images of another time and another place. But the fact is that the sport of rowing is as important on the Potomac as it ever was on the Thames in London. Georgetown University, George Washington, Trinity, and Navy all compete here, and the 250-member Boat Club sponsors three major regattas each year. Four of its members competed in the 1980 Olympics. (Fred J. Maroon)

118–119 ✦ One of the District's most prestigious neighborhoods, Foggy Bottom was once the site of a factory that made illuminating gas as well as dozens of breweries. The working-class people who lived there called it Funkstown. Its new name came from the vapors that seemed to be constantly rising from the swamp that was replaced by the Lincoln Memorial. It got its prestige when the State Department moved there after World War II. (Fred Ward)

120–121 ✦ Washington's original architect, Pierre Charles L'Enfant, had grown up in the gardens of Versailles, where his father was a painter at the French royal court. Though many of his dreams were never realized, his hope for making Washington the most beautiful of all the world capitals inspired designers who followed him. And there are days when even Paris pales by comparison. (Fred J. Maroon)

122–123 ✦ Their moms surely told these kids not to get their feet wet, but that's like trying to talk back the tide. Wet feet are part of the fun at Hains Point, the eastern tip of East Potomac Park and the District's first park built on a reclaimed swamp. On most days the rail is lined with fishermen. And when summer heat gets oppressive, the walk is full of strollers who know that this is the coolest spot in Washington. In September, Hains Point is the best place in town to watch the President's Cup Regatta in the Potomac Channel. (William S. Weems)

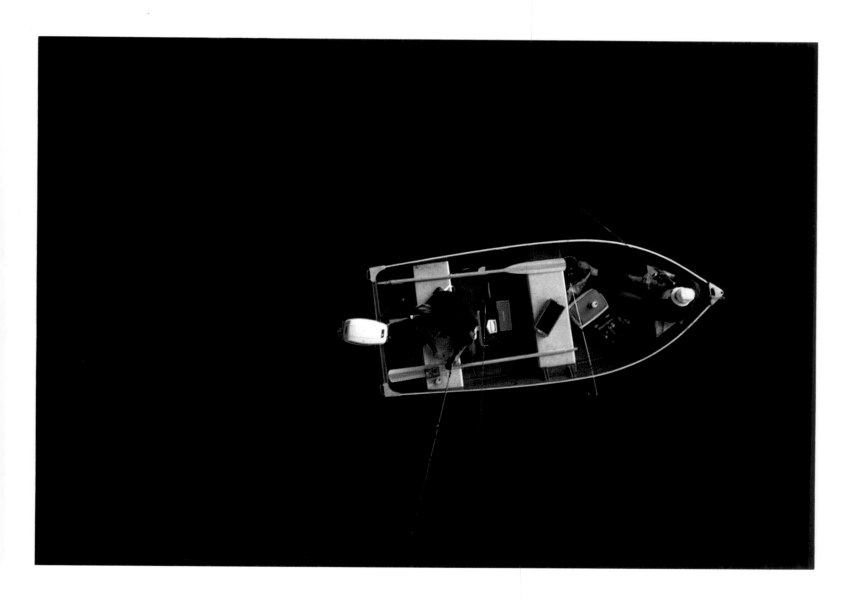

124 ◆ In 1977, when he discovered that it was costing the government $800,000 a year to keep the Presidential yacht, *Sequoia*, afloat, President Jimmy Carter ordered the 104-foot craft sold to the highest bidder. The highest bid turned out to be $286,000, about $110,000 more than it had cost to have her built. Every President since Herbert Hoover had used a yacht for relaxing and entertaining on the waters of the Potomac. But if the Ship of State is the only thing left for a President to command, his neighbors in the District make do with smaller pleasures on lazy Sunday afternoons. (Jonathan Wallen)

125 ◆ On a weekday you can rent a rowboat or a canoe in Georgetown and spend an hour on the Potomac for less than $5. If you stay out all day, the fee is less than $10. The rates are slightly higher on holidays and weekends, but only slightly. Where else can you find such a perfect way to get away from it all with such a small investment? (Kay Chernush)

126–127 ◆ Any time of day, any time of year, people line the Potomac riverbank in the shadow of the Georgetown University spires and drop fishing lines into the water. It's one of the area's most popular sports, but present-day anglers have trouble believing Captain John Smith's 1608 report of his first Potomac exploration. "There is an abundance of fish," he wrote, "lying so thick with their backs above the water. . . . Neither better fish, more plenty, nor variety had any of us seen in any stream." He also reported catching them with a frying pan. But that may be a fish story. (Fred J. Maroon)

128–129 ◆ The U.S. Marine Corps Band and other military units, as well as the D.C. Recreation Department Symphony Orchestra, give free performances at the Watergate on the Potomac near the Lincoln Memorial every night except Monday and Saturday from June through August. The music lovers who come to listen to the open-air concerts sit on stone bleachers, but many find it more romantic to rent a canoe and slip under the platform out of sight of the musicians. (Fred J. Maroon)

AUDIENCES

Ask a politician what's more important than anything else and the answer might well be "an audience." There are plenty of them in Washington, and often politicians are part of them because there is much more to listen to here than speeches. There are more places for audiences to gather than in most cities, too.

130 ◆ Grover Cleveland's second inauguration in 1893 made him the 24th President. He had already been the 22d, but his two terms were not consecutive.

131 ◆ "We are fifty-three Americans who will always have a love affair with this country," said L. Bruce Laingen, spokesman for the fifty-two newly released former hostages home from Iran and joined on the White House lawn by another who had been released earlier. They were also joined by some six thousand government employees and other dignitaries, including President and Mrs. Ronald Reagan, who, on January 27, 1981, were at the end of their first week in the White House. (Enrico Ferorelli)

132–133 ◆ The Robert F. Kennedy Memorial Stadium on the banks of the Anacostia River can pack in fifty-five thousand fans to watch the Washington Redskins play professional football. All that excitement usually makes them hungry, which is good news for the people who sell hot dogs there. The Skins' overall record in the National Football League is a bit dismal, but their home games are almost always sold out. As the late Red Smith pointed out in one of his last *New York Times* columns: "Nowhere else does the game seem to touch the life of the community as it does in Washington. The whole town seems to sag when the Redskins lose." (Fred J. Maroon)

134 ✦ The U.S. Marine Corps Band started it all in 1801. Much later General Pershing ordered that the Army should have its own band to stir the doughboys in World War I. The Navy got into the act in 1923, and the Air Force had its own band by the time it became independent of the Army in 1947. But summer sounds also include symphonic music in free concerts like this one at the Capitol. (Jonathan Wallen)

135 ✦ Critics used words like "dowdy" to describe the National Symphony before the Soviet cellist, Mstislav Rostropovich, became its musical director in 1977. Since then it has made many recordings, taken its first trip abroad, and regularly performed to sell-out audiences at the Kennedy Center. When they appear at outdoor concerts like this one, crowds arrive early; many wear lavender Rostropovich T-shirts and speculate about whether "Slava," as the Maestro is called, will appear with his miniature dachshund, Pooka, under his arm. (Kelly/Mooney)

136 ✦ The Metropolitan AME Church is the "connectional" church for the million-member African Methodist Episcopal Church in the United States. The building, opened in 1881, has a second-floor sanctuary supported by outside bearing walls, leaving the interior free of columns. Rooms under its basement were an important stop in the underground railroad for slaves escaping to freedom. Among its parishioners, Paul Lawrence Dunbar, the poet, and Frederick Douglass, who became Minister to Haiti, are honored with memorials in the church. (Jeff Perkell)

137 ✦ The most important rooms in the Rayburn House Office Building are its nine hearing rooms. Important in terms of history, that is. Some representatives whose office suites are in this $86-million building might prefer the gymnasium, or the swimming pool, or their offices, one of 169 doled out on the basis of seniority. Less senior members of the House of Representatives have offices in the 1908 Cannon Building or the 1933 Longworth Building. When the Rayburn Building was opened in 1965, *New York Times* architecture critic Ada Louise Huxtable said it was an achievement because it was "both dull and vulgar." (Jeff Perkell)

138–139 ✦ Every four years, everyone who can goes to the Capitol to watch the outdoor ceremony of the swearing-in of the President. Important officials, including formally dressed members of Congress, get to sit in a place of honor. And why not? Congress pays the bill, which for the 1981 ceremony of the inauguration of President Reagan came to $450,000. Other frills, like the parade and the inaugural balls, were extra. (Fred Ward/Black Star)

140–141 ✦ On October 1, 1979, Pope John Paul II began a six-thousand-mile pilgrimage to six American cities by celebrating mass at the Boston Common. A week later, on October 7, he ended the tour with a mass on the Mall, which had been visited earlier in the year by another of the world's great religious leaders, the Dalai Lama. According to some reports, the crowd that appeared on the Mall to see and hear the Pope was the biggest since the day President Monroe welcomed the Marquis de Lafayette here in 1824. (Mike Mitchell)

THE LINCOLN MEMORIAL

There are few monuments anywhere in the world that can boast the inspiring nobility of the Lincoln Memorial. It is easily the most impressive in Washington, reflecting the spirit of the man it honors in an almost perfect way. The architect, Henry Bacon, said that he also wanted it to be "a symbol of the Union of the United States, which Abraham Lincoln stated it was his paramount object to save . . . and which he did save." What Bacon and sculptor Daniel Chester French created is an emotional experience that never fails to touch all who visit here.

142 ✦ During his transcontinental tour of the United States in 1959, Soviet Premier Nikita Khrushchev learned something of America at the Lincoln Memorial. (Burt Glinn/Magnum)

143 ✦ If he were standing, Mr. Lincoln would be twenty-eight feet tall, about half the height of the main chamber. Though the sculpture appears to be carved from a single piece of stone, it is actually composed of twenty blocks of Georgia marble, all perfectly interlocked. It took the Picirilli Brothers stonecutters four years to build the figure from Daniel Chester French's model. It took Congress almost fifty years to decide what form a memorial to Lincoln should take. (William S. Weems)

144 ♦ This is the second sculpture of Lincoln by the great Daniel Chester French. The other is a standing figure, ten years older, in Lincoln, Nebraska. When this face was unveiled, a British critic said it was the finest likeness he had ever seen and that the only one that even approached it was one he saw somewhere in Nebraska by an artist whose name he had forgotten. (Steven Gottlieb)

145 ♦ Each of the thirty-six fluted columns that enclose the monument is 44 feet high and 7 feet 5 inches around. They represent the number of states in the union at the time of Lincoln's death in 1865, five days after the end of the Civil War. The names of those states are inscribed in a frieze above the columns. On the parapet outside, forty-eight festoons signify the number of states in the union at the time the Lincoln Memorial was dedicated in 1922. A recent proposal to add two more to honor Alaska and Hawaii was defeated in Congress. (Nicholas Foster)

146 ♦ Though this sculpture has been seen and praised by more people than any other work by Daniel Chester French, his own favorite was a figure of a soldier standing in a park in Milton, Massachusetts. The one that made him famous is the 1875 statue of the Minute Man that stands on the Village Green in Concord, Massachusetts, French's hometown. In World War II, the figure became the symbol of the effort to raise funds through the sale of war bonds and stamps. (Steven Gottlieb)

147 ♦ Even at noon on a cloudless day, special lighting inside the Memorial insures the right effect of shadow on the sculpture, no matter when you see it. It was seen by the public for the first time on May 30, 1922, when it was dedicated by President Warren G. Harding. "It is estimated that 50,000 persons heard the exercises . . . made possible by the use of loudspeakers so the addresses were distinctly heard in the remotest parts of the grounds," said *The New York Times*. What *The Times* didn't say was that the audience was segregated. Blacks were confined to the other side of the road. (Michael D. Sullivan)

148–149 ♦ All the monuments are washed down periodically to get rid of accumulated dust and spider webs. But Mr. Lincoln gets a bath twice a year, in the spring and fall, with water from high-pressure hoses and a mild detergent. The combination of exhaust from cars and buses, and the fallout from jets flying into National Airport, is causing a problem that makes constant maintenance vital. Referring to deterioration of the Colorado Yule marble on the exterior of the Memorial, a restoration expert said: "It is like a giant Alka-Seltzer tablet. You can almost hear it fizz when it rains." (Jonathan Wallen)

150–151 ♦ Ice skaters on the frozen reflecting pool go right on making their figure eights while a memorial ceremony honoring Dr. Martin Luther King takes place behind them. In the spring of 1939, thousands gathered at this spot to hear a recital by contralto Marian Anderson, who chose the Lincoln Memorial as an alternative to Constitution Hall whose doors were closed to her because of her race. (Fred J. Maroon)

WINTER

On average, the coldest month of the year in Washington is January, but even then the temperature is above freezing. But don't talk to Washingtonians about averages. Back in 1922, a 24-hour snowstorm dumped twenty-five inches of snow on the District, more than half of what Bostonians have to shovel away in an average year. Winter in Washington is best described as damp, slushy, and slightly depressing. But it can be beautiful, too. And it is easily the most exciting time of the year.

152 ◆ Andrew Jackson had been in Lafayette Square for eighty years when this picture was taken of the North Front of the White House in the early 1930's.

153 ◆ If you overstay your welcome at a Washington parking meter, whatever the reason, you'll probably find a ticket on your windshield when you get back. The fine for a simple violation like that is $10, but as violations get more serious, so do the fines for, as the Metropolitan Police describe it, "impeding rush hour traffic." If you stay away too long from an illegally parked car, it might not be there when you get back. If a police tow truck takes it away, add $50 to the cost of the ticket. (Michael D. Sullivan)

154–155 ◆ The grand system of grids, diagonals, and open spaces that makes Washington the envy of other great cities is never more evident than with a dusting of light snow. Even though planners of every stripe have put their mark on the city since the 1791 L'Enfant plan was accepted, the original is still evident. Probably because it works so well. (James A. Sugar)

156–157 ◆ Except for the statue of England's George III, angrily removed from New York's Bowling Green to make Revolutionary War cannonballs, this sculpture of Andrew Jackson in Lafayette Park is America's first equestrian statue. It was cast in 1853 by Clark Mills from bronze cannons captured by Jackson in the War of 1812. According to an unwritten rule, statues placed in circles around town always faced the White House. This one doesn't, which is why, they say, he is tipping his hat to the Executive Mansion. (John Neubauer)

158 ◆ The Algonquin Indians who lived here before the Europeans came used their canoes all year. So did the trappers for whom the Potomac was one of their routes to the West. Today canoes are considered good only for summer fun and are stacked on the Georgetown shore during the cold months. The Indian settlements in this area were among the first to vanish. As Thomas Jefferson recorded, in the sixty years following the first English settlement in Virginia "two-thirds of the Indians disappeared because of smallpox, spirituous liquors and abridgement of territory." (Roger Foley)

159 ◆ There are no stairways in any of the stations of the Metro system, only escalators. They include some of the longest in the world and some of the very few that operate outdoors in all kinds of weather. The escalators are controlled by separate motors for each twenty feet of their length. The weight of the passengers on the steps causes the motors to turn on and off as needed. (Everett C. Johnson/Lensman)

160–161 ◆ The gardens and terraces of Dumbarton Oaks in Georgetown were designed by Beatrix Ferrand for Robert Woods Bliss, a career diplomat who owned the estate from 1920 to 1940. It is now the property of Harvard University, which uses funds endowed by Bliss to continue and enlarge his library devoted to Byzantine studies, Pre-Columbian art, and landscape gardening. The sixteen-acre garden is usually open to the public on weekends and to students by appointment. (William S. Weems)

162–163 ◆ "I don't want it torn down," said Harry S. Truman, "it's the greatest monstrosity in America." The great monstrosity is the Old State, War, and Navy Building on Pennsylvania Avenue next to the White House. Its ten acres of floor space house some of the President's staff as well as the Office of Management and Budget. Today, this 1888 building goes by the less exciting name of Executive Office Building. This view of it is from across the avenue, from a bedroom in Blair House used by visiting heads of state, royalty, and important foreign officials. (Fred J. Maroon)

164–165 ◆ The community of Georgetown became an official entity in 1741 and instantly became one of the area's wealthiest communities thanks to the ships it sent down the Potomac loaded with tobacco and other treasures bound for Europe. Some of the structures the ship owners and planters built were showplaces then and they still are. But most of Georgetown's historic houses were built in the style of their predecessors in the late 1800's. They're beautiful at any time of year, but a fresh winter snow adds a special touch. (Fred J. Maroon)

EXTERIORS

The buildings in Washington are Classical, Baroque, Victorian, Contemporary. In fact, every style that was ever fashionable in the United States is represented in some form or other. But the result is less of a hodgepodge than some architectural critics might suggest. The bricks are redder, the marble whiter than in other places. The open space around most buildings prevents open hostility between competing styles. But if it is a city without a typical style of its own, it is still very much the City Beautiful.

166 ◆ The Post Office Building on Pennsylvania Avenue was still under construction when the Labor Day parade passed by in 1894.

167 ◆ The high iron content of the clay in the area makes the brick fronts of Washington houses a lot redder than their counterparts in other Colonial cities. Washington's best Colonial feeling is in Georgetown, where residents work hard at keeping it that way. But the city has hundreds of comfortable brick row houses in other neighborhoods, many with projecting bay windows and landscaped lawns separating them from streets that are eighty feet wide. Most of them were built in the 1880's, but some are as new as the 1920's. (Howard Millard)

168–169 ◆ The flags of the United States and of Venezuela in front of the Executive Office Building honor a three-day state visit by Venezuela's President Luis Herrera Campins in November 1981. (Jeff Perkell)

170–171 ◆ When I. M. Pei was given the commission for the East Building of the National Gallery of Art, he was also given a few restraints. It had to complement the West Building and was not to be an inch higher. He made it a foot lower; the towers are 108 feet above the ground. He went to the same Tennessee marble quarry Alexander Pope had used for the older building so the materials would be sure to match, and then he lined up his triangular design with the center of the original gallery. (Howard Millard)

172 ◆ Especially in winter, the setting sun gives the Capitol dome, and buildings all over town, a very special glow. Once that show is over, human technology begins and the dome is floodlit until dawn. As far back as 1867, an elaborate system of oil lamps illuminated the dome on nights when Congress was in session. During the day, flags over the Senate and House Chambers are a signal that work is being done inside, but the lighting was considered necessary after dark when the flags couldn't be seen. Today, a light at the very top of the dome signals that Congress is in night session. (Jeff Perkell)

173 ◆ The Arts and Industries Building, one of seven Smithsonian buildings on the Mall, was constructed to house more than sixty freight cars full of exhibits and artifacts that had been gathered for the 1876 Centennial Exposition in Philadelphia. Its $250,000 cost makes it a contender for the honor of being the cheapest public building that the Federal government has ever built. (Marianne Bernstein)

174 ◆ A castle on the Rhine? No, a castle on the Mall—James Renwick's Smithsonian castle. As the first city in the history of the world created only to be the seat of government, Washington became the laughing-stock of sophisticated Europeans far into the nineteenth century because there was so much empty space between the buildings. As Charles Dickens put it in 1842: "One might fancy the season over and most of the houses gone out of town with their masters." Washington people just smiled and bided their time. (Kay Chernush)

175 ◆ Looking at this building at 17th and H Street, it's hard to imagine that it would ever be confused with the French Empire pile next door to the White House, but they both have almost the same name. This is the *New* Executive Office Building, which houses many of the President's top advisors behind its forbidding brick walls and narrow windows. (David Robinson)

176 ◆ The Greek Revival Treasury Building, built in the late 1830's, is adorned with Ionic columns on its east front. On the other side of the building, an exhibit of some of the nation's fiscal artifacts includes a check for $7.2 million paid to Russia for the Territory of Alaska. In yet another part, some of the country's silver and gold reserves are stored in special vaults guarded by the Secret Service, a Treasury division. (Mike Mitchell)

177 ◆ The Administration Building of the Blue Plains Sewage Treatment Center isn't one of the regular stops on the standard sightseeing tour of Washington, but it's worth a look. Like a huge corncrib, it is wider at the top than at the foundation line. (Mike Mitchell)

178–179 ◆ Things are not always what they seem in Washington. A casual stroller coming around this corner would swear that the building with a tall smokestack has to be a factory. It was. But now it is an apartment house, and the neighborhood its chimney dominates is considered one of the most desirable in town, on the banks of the C&O Canal in Georgetown. (Kay Chernush)

180–181 ◆ One of the best neighborhoods in town for good restaurants is around 19th and M Street NW, where this glass facade reflects a Washington favorite, Gusti's Italian Restaurant. It has ten different dining rooms inside, and in the summer it adds an eleventh out in the front yard. There is no better place in the entire District for people-watching. The pizza is pretty good, too. (Michael Hoyt/Lensman)

Northwestern Federal Savings and Loan Association

Northwestern Federal Savings and Loan Association

CELEBRATIONS

There is always something to celebrate in Washington, from Benjamin Franklin's birthday in January right through to Christmas. And there are always plenty of people to share the excitement. The year begins with a dozen or more official dinners and receptions at the White House during January and February. Embassies celebrate their own national holidays, and we celebrate ours in July with the most impressive show in the country. Celebrations take place in churches, parks, historic sites, anywhere at all. It adds a quality to Washington life that not many other cities can match.

182 ✦ The Fourth of July, 1934, as photographed with a bellows camera by Theodor Horydczak who stood under a black drape to snap the shutter.

183 ✦ One of the eighty-eight works that were part of the 11th International Sculpture Conference in June 1980, a laser installation by local artist Rockne Krebs was so popular it was kept in place most of the summer and provided a perfect counterpoint for the Fourth of July fireworks display on the Mall. Two lasers at the base of the Lincoln Memorial were refracted from the top of it past the Washington Monument toward the Capitol. Two more at the Jefferson Memorial formed a crisscross pattern with them and sent beams to the White House and beyond. It was the artist's intent to unite the city's landmarks and reinforce the plan of the Mall. (Jeff Wilkes)

184–185 ✦ Visiting dignitaries traditionally place a wreath at the Tomb of the Unknowns in Arlington National Cemetery. When they do, they themselves are saluted with cannon fire. Royalty and heads of state are saluted with twenty-one blasts of black powder from the muzzles of these 75mm guns, known as "French 75s." Lesser officials rate fewer shots, ranging from nineteen for the next lower level to eleven for consuls general. The salutes are fired in other places, too, and the guns are moved from place to place on 105mm howitzer caissons. (Henri Dauman)

186 ✦ The diplomatic community in Washington is made up of well over ten thousand persons from some hundred fifteen countries. There are more than two hundred fifty correspondents from foreign news-gathering organizations and countless thousands of other foreign nationals here for one reason or another. They often turn out to join in local celebrations and frequently use the occasion to do a little flag-waving of their own. (Fred J. Maroon)

187 ✦ Uncle Sam is the biggest single employer in the United States with a nationwide total of employees about equal to the population of the city of Chicago. But the biggest concentration of Uncle Sam's dependent nieces and nephews, upwards of a half-million of them, is, naturally, right here in Washington. It's only fitting that he should participate in their celebrations such as the Independence Day Parade. (Fred J. Maroon)

188–189 ✦ Every fourth year, on January 20, Pennsylvania Avenue is the scene of one of the country's biggest parades, celebrating the inauguration of the President. But just for the fun of it, there are other parades at other times like this one in Georgetown. Washington traditionally celebrates Army Day in April, Memorial Day in May, Independence Day in July, and both Navy Day and Halloween in October by staging spectacular parades. (Fred J. Maroon)

190–191 ✦ Back in 1783, when Congress was meeting in Philadelphia, a group that looked just like this one descended on them demanding back pay. Congress answered them by moving to Princeton, New Jersey. Present-day Congressmen didn't seem as perturbed when these gentlemen appeared in Washington's Fourth of July parade. (Paul Conklin)

192 ✦ The Islamic Center and its mosque, the only air-conditioned mosque in the United States, were designed by Mario Rossi, an Italian architect whose fascination with the old mosques of Cairo led him to become a convert to Islam. The Center was created by ambassadors representing forty major Islamic countries in Washington. It functions as a clearing house for information on worship for more than two million Moslems living in the United States. (Steven Gottlieb)

193 ✦ When Pope John Paul II celebrated mass on the Mall, in October 1979, a special altar was constructed for the occasion. Less than a week before, a lawsuit in Federal District Court sought to block the construction and the mass itself on grounds of "excessive entanglement" between Church and State. Fortunately, the judge refused to block it and the altar was ready in time. Meanwhile, the plaintiff, Madalyn Murray O'Hair, went to Chicago to lead a protest against a Papal outdoor mass in Grant Park. (Mike Mitchell)

194 ✦ For generations, black Americans were denied the traditional trappings of organized religion and so they created their own in which highly charged emotions were released. That tradition is still very much alive in storefront churches like the Christian Tabernacle Church of God, Inc., on Georgia Avenue, whose minister, Rev. William F. Hart, like so many of his colleagues, is forced to support himself by working at another job during the week. (Sidney A. Tabak)

195 ✦ Except for the Cherry Blossom Festival, the most popular rite of spring in Washington is the annual Easter Egg Roll on the White House lawn. But not everyone is welcome. Until 1970, to be admitted to the grounds you had to be under twelve years old, or be with someone who was. Then the age limit was lowered to eight, but that didn't cut down the crowds. Finding Easter eggs is the object of the game, but most participants find time to be photographed with the Easter Bunny, preferably with the White House in the background.
(William S. Weems)

196 ✦ If you've ever wondered what the President and his family see when they look out from the White House, this is one of the views. Especially at Christmas time, when the festive lights inside are reflected in the windowpanes and the Washington Monument is complemented by Christmas trees outdoors on the Ellipse, it's clearly one of the nice things about being the Chief Executive. (Fred J. Maroon)

197 ✦ Of all the decisions a President is expected to make, the one about how the White House ought to be decorated for Christmas is traditionally delegated to his wife, the First Lady. This Victorian theme was selected by Rosalynn Carter in 1980, her last year there. The official White House Christmas tree, in the Blue Room, was surrounded by four Victorian dollhouses. This one was the first that visitors saw when they entered the room. In her first year as First Lady, Mrs. Carter used decorations made for the occasion by handicapped people in workshops around the country. (Fred J. Maroon)

THE MALL

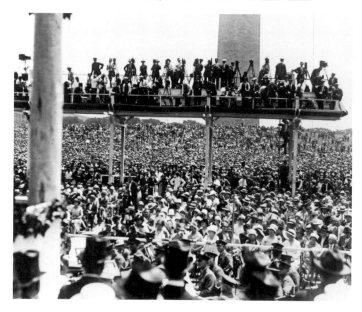

The original idea had been a sweep of open space from the Capitol to the river, but along the way the plans were changed. A creek that cut across it overflowed at high tide, so a canal was dug to contain it. The Baltimore and Potomac Railroad built a passenger station on it and laid tracks across it. A plan ordered by President Millard Fillmore turned some of it into a nature preserve. In 1902, Michigan Senator James McMillan submitted a plan calling for a return to basics. The railroad station went, the canal was filled in, and marshland along the river was converted to solid ground. The restoration began in 1910 and was capped by the Jefferson Memorial in 1942.

198 ✦ In June 1927, the most important man in Washington was Charles A. Lindbergh, just back from Paris. These people gave him the welcome he deserved here on the Mall.

199 ✦ Nearly all the 750 acres of Washington National Airport, across the Potomac from the central city, is landfill held back from the river by more than two miles of levee. There was room left over for playing fields where soccer players have never been known to kick about the noise from passing jets. There are a half-dozen municipal soccer fields on the other side of the river, too, providing plenty of competing teams. The competition gets especially fierce at the end of the season when they have play-off tournaments for local championships. (William S. Weems)

200–201 ✦ One night in 1854, not long after the sun had set on the unfinished Washington Monument, a band of men representing a political party called the "Know-Nothings" overpowered the watchman and made off with a block of stone that had been sent here from Rome by Pope Pius IX. It was never recovered, and the idea of building the monument from donated blocks of marble was dropped. Congress didn't appropriate money to buy marble until twenty-two years later, and during those years the monument was nothing more than a 156-foot stump. (Kay Chernush)

202–203 ✦ The grassy area between Independence Avenue and Ohio Drive, just west of the Tidal Basin, becomes a polo field every Sunday afternoon from April through July and from September through November. About thirty-five of the members of the National Capital Polo Association participate in matches against teams from Virginia, the Carolinas, and Pennsylvania. Every second year they host an American tour by the British Army Combined Services Polo Group, and in the years in between they send their own team to England. There is space enough for about four hundred spectators to watch them on the Mall, usually without charge. The Association sponsors other fund-raising events to help the Parks Service maintain the area. (John Neubauer)

204–205 ✦ The Smithsonian's transportation collection includes a gleaming steam locomotive, an authentic stagecoach, and a Conestoga wagon. It has a 1920 Mack truck and a 1903 Cadillac, too, but just for the fun of it, it also has a conveyance that doesn't go anywhere at all: a wonderful carrousel just outside on the Mall. (Steven Gottlieb)

206 ✦ Eating out in Washington can be a stimulating adventure and, thanks to an unusually large number of cafeterias, not always an expensive one. But on a nice day at noon the grassy spaces in the parks and on the Mall resemble sidewalk cafés when thousands of office workers arrive with brown-bagged lunches in search of a little sun, a little relaxation, a little romance. (Jonathan Wallen)

207 ✦ The old Pan-American Union Building, built in 1910 mostly with money donated by Andrew Carnegie, is now called the OAS Building, shorthand for its occupant, the Organization of American States. A room inside, the Hall of the Americas, has chandeliers designed by Louis Comfort Tiffany, which help to make it one of the city's most beautiful spaces. Its Spanish Colonial exterior forms a backdrop to colorful jousting matches held near it on the Mall every year. It also adds a romantic touch to almost any scene. (John Neubauer)

208–209 ✦ Japanese artist Fujiko Nakaya's contribution to the 11th International Sculpture Conference, held in Washington in 1980, was a steam sculpture on the grounds of the U.S. Botanic Garden. A steam generator was buried under the earth, and the pattern of steam rising apparently out of nowhere varied with the changing breeze. Steam has been piped into the Botanic Garden's conservatory since 1938, making it possible to grow and exhibit more than five hundred types of orchids. (Don Hamerman)

DUSK

In the opinion of people in other parts of the country, the setting sun is a signal for the Washington establishment to begin making the rounds of the cocktail party circuit. There are parties, to be sure. But in a town where what you said tonight will probably be remembered tomorrow morning, the liquor bills for Washington hosts are surprisingly low. Who gets invited to the best parties in town depends on who they're close to. Knowing the President is best, but any other legitimate source of power will do. People who aren't "in" right now can always wait for the next election. Meanwhile, the beautiful sunsets offer a certain consolation.

210 ✦ A rainy night outside the Capitol Building in 1930.

211 ✦ More than a dozen airlines carry passengers in and out of Washington National Airport, just three-and-a-half miles from the center of town. It was built as a WPA project beginning in 1938 and formally opened in 1940. Dulles International Airport, twenty-seven miles and a $30 cab ride outside Washington at Chantilly, Virginia, was opened in 1962 to handle the big jets that found Washington National a bit cramped. Friendship International Airport, just south of Baltimore, has been renamed Baltimore-Washington International Airport, but it's more than thirty miles away from the Washington Monument.
(Marvin E. Newman)

212 ◆ Right now, wouldn't soft shell crabs hit the spot? When they're in season, you can get them fresh from the Chesapeake Bay along the Maine Avenue waterfront and what a treat that is! All year, the Maine Avenue stalls and stores feature the freshest fish in town, everything from bluefish that were swimming in the Bay this morning to catfish from the nearby tidewater. What are you waiting for? Tonight's dinner is right there. (Sally DiMartini)

213 ◆ When the Department of Commerce Building was finished in 1932, it was the biggest office building in Washington. Its six sections, each enclosing an inner courtyard, cover an area one block wide and three blocks long. If they were stacked on top of each other, the building would be forty-two stories high. People who work there keep in shape by walking through its eight miles of corridors, but there are thirty-two elevators so they don't have to climb too many stairs. When the lights in the building go out, the Census Clock in the lobby continues flashing, keeping track of our growing population. (Fred J. Maroon)

214–215 ◆ The neighborhood around Dupont Circle was once considered the best address in Washington by the nineteenth-century super-rich. Their influence was so great that streetcar tracks skirted around it so residents wouldn't be disturbed. Many of the mansions there have been converted to embassies, clubs, or institutions, but nearby houses like these on R Street are still wonderful places to live. Young people make the Circle itself one of the city's most vibrant meeting places. (Michael D. Sullivan)

216–217 ◆ When Franklin D. Roosevelt brought the New Deal to Washington in 1933, he also introduced a new breed to the bureaucracy: the commuter. The first suburb they discovered was Alexandria, Virginia, nine miles south of Washington, which is where this traveling carnival caught up with them. In the fifty years since they moved in, Alexandria hasn't changed much more than it did in the hundred-fifty years before that. Back in 1933, though, the original Alexandrians didn't know what to expect of the newcomers, whom they called "the Foreign Legion." By now they knew they had nothing to fear but fear itself. (John Neubauer)

218–219 ◆ The rotunda of the Jefferson Memorial is in the style of the Pantheon in Rome, as is the Rotunda of the University of Virginia, designed by the third President himself. Before it was officially opened, in April 1943, Washington women banded together to protest the removal of cherry trees to make room for it. Some even chained themselves to the trees to make uprooting harder. President Franklin D. Roosevelt added insult to injury by having a swath of trees cut between the White House and the Tidal Basin so he could watch the progress of construction. (Kay Chernush)

220–221 ◆ A decade before the Lincoln Memorial was placed at the end of the Mall, the area was mostly swampland. During the debate that preceded construction, Speaker of the House Joe Cannon said: "Don't put the memorial here, boys. Why, the malarial ague from these mosquitoes would shake it to pieces." Fortunately he didn't convince his colleagues. It's hard to imagine a better site, especially when it's framed by a summer sunset. (Steven Gottlieb)

222–223 ◆ Almost any night at the White House is a memorable occasion, but the night that the lighting sculptor Joe Strand and photographer Dudley Gray showed up, with a crew of fourteen and a van full of heavy lights, is one the staff will never forget. In their three months of planning, they relied on five years of experience of specially lighting bridges, buildings, and monuments. Here they determined that they would need 600 amps of power, enough for 100,000 watts of light, which they found available in outlets scattered around the White House lawn. It took five hours to set up the colored lights and more than an hour to photograph the result of their work while building electricians crossed their fingers in hopes they wouldn't blow a Presidential fuse. (Dudley Gray)

INDEX OF PHOTOGRAPHERS

All photographs are copyrighted in the following photographers' names:

Aikens, John 99
Bernstein, Marianne 173
Brimberg, Marie L. 4–5
Brown, Stephen 56
Bullaty, Sonja 69
Chernush, Kay 14–15, 59, 92–93, 125, 174, 178–79, 200–201, 218–19
Colbroth, Ron 51
Conklin, Paul 95, 190–91
Dauman, Henri 184–85
DiMartini, Sally 58, 212
Edwards, Gregory 8–9
Evans, Michael 114
Ferorelli, Enrico 73, 131
Fishman, Chuck 26–27
Foley, Roger 158
Foster, Nicholas 111, 145
Garrett, Kenneth 28–29
Glinn, Burt 142
Gottlieb, Steven 57, 144, 146, 192, 204–205, 220–21
Gray, Dudley 222–23
Hamerman, Don 6–7, 68, 208–209, jacket
Hirshfeld, Max 60–61
Hoyt, Michael 180–81
Jean-Bart, Leslie 18–19
Johnson, Cynthia 115
Johnson, Everett C. 159
Karales, James H. 101
Kelly/Mooney 135
Lippman, Richard 108–109
Maroon, Fred J. 2–3, 22–23, 24–25, 72, 100, 102, 112–13, 117, 120–21, 126–27, 128–29, 132–33, 150–51, 162–63, 164–65, 186, 187, 188–89, 196, 197, 213
McGrail, John 30–31, 63
Millard, Howard 35–38, 103, 167, 170–71
Mitchell, Mike 54–55, 140–41, 176, 177, 193
Neubauer, John 20–21, 98, 156–57, 202–203, 207, 216–17
Newman, Marvin E. 79, 83, 211
Perkell, Jeff 77, 136, 137, 168–69, 172
Robinson, David 175
Sherbell, Shepard 90, 91
Slavin, Neal 110
Sugar, James A. (Woodfin-Camp) 154–55
Sullivan, Michael D. 88–89, 147, 153, 214–15
Tabak, Sidney A. 66–67, 194
Wallen, Jonathan 1, 10–11, 12–13, 16–17, 64–65, 71, 80, 81, 82, 86–87, 96–97, 124, 134, 148–49, 206
Ward, Fred 32–33, 74–75, 78, 107, 118–19, 138–39
Webb, Alex 84–85
Weems, William S. (Woodfin-Camp) 50, 52–53, 70, 104–105, 122–23, 143, 160–61, 195, 199
Wilkes, Jeff 183

Acknowledgments
Collection Architect of the Capitol 45
Collection Kathy Hall McMullan 49
Collection Library of Congress 44, 45 bottom, 46, 47 top, 48, 62, 76, 94, 106, 116, 130, 152, 166, 182, 198, 210
Mark Segal, 46–47

Text Editor: Nora Beeson

First Edition

LIBRARY OF CONGRESS CATALOGING IN PUBLICATION DATA
Main entry under title:

Washington, D.C.

1. Washington (D.C.)—Description—1981–   —Views.
I. Suarès, Jean-Claude. II. Harris, Bill, 1933–
F195.W63   975.3'04   82-3925
ISBN 0-8109-1787-4   AACR2

© 1982 J.-C. Suarès
Text © 1982 Bill Harris